50 Cooking in the Dark Dishes

By: Kelly Johnson

Table of Contents

- Midnight Blackout Stew
- Shadowy Smoked Brisket
- Dark Chocolate Chili
- Black Garlic Butter Chicken
- Mystery Meatloaf
- Pitch-Black Squid Ink Pasta
- Hidden Ingredient Casserole
- Twilight Truffle Risotto
- Charcoal-Grilled Lamb Chops
- Obsidian Glazed Ribs
- Nocturnal Mushroom Soup
- Phantom Pepper Stir-Fry
- Secret Spice Meatballs
- Dusky Bourbon-Braised Short Ribs
- Starlit Black Bean Burgers
- Cloaked-in-Darkness Beef Stew
- Enigma Eggplant Parmesan
- Blackened Cajun Salmon
- Deep Midnight Pot Roast
- Hidden Heat Tandoori Chicken
- Shadowy Smoked Mac & Cheese
- Eclipse Espresso BBQ Chicken
- Forbidden Rice & Coconut Curry
- Smoldering Ember Meat Pie
- Midnight Market Noodle Bowl
- Candied Bacon Mystery Bites
- Sable-Spiced Lentil Soup
- Moonlit Moroccan Tagine
- Dark Roast Coffee-Rubbed Steak
- Dusky Plum-Glazed Duck
- Pitch-Black Charcoal Pizza
- Unknown Depths Seafood Gumbo
- Sinister Smoked Pork Shoulder
- Shrouded in Smoke BBQ Wings
- Cloaked Cauliflower Mash

- Hidden Treasure Jambalaya
- Silent Night Szechuan Noodles
- Dark Honey-Glazed Ham
- Mystery Mushroom Stroganoff
- Veiled Vanilla-Balsamic Chicken
- Black Bean & Chorizo Enchiladas
- Mysterious Midnight Lasagna
- Obscured in Darkness Ramen
- Shadowy Shepherd's Pie
- Deep Night Bourbon Caramel Pork
- Masquerade Meat & Cheese Fondue
- Lurking Lobster Bisque
- Blindfolded Brown Butter Gnocchi
- Hidden Hands Spicy Curry
- Secret Smokehouse Brisket

Midnight Blackout Stew

Ingredients:

- 500g beef chuck, cubed
- 1 tbsp olive oil
- 1 onion, chopped
- 3 garlic cloves, minced
- 2 tbsp tomato paste
- 500ml dark stout beer
- 500ml beef broth
- 1 can (400g) black beans, drained
- 2 carrots, chopped
- 1 tbsp Worcestershire sauce
- 1 tsp smoked paprika
- ½ tsp black pepper
- Salt to taste

Instructions:

1. Heat oil in a pot and brown beef. Remove and set aside.
2. Sauté onion and garlic until soft.
3. Stir in tomato paste, then add beer and broth.
4. Return beef to the pot and add remaining ingredients.
5. Simmer for 2 hours until tender.

Shadowy Smoked Brisket

Ingredients:

- 2kg beef brisket
- 2 tbsp black pepper
- 1 tbsp smoked salt
- 1 tbsp garlic powder
- 1 tbsp onion powder
- 1 tbsp smoked paprika
- 1 tsp cayenne pepper
- 1 cup beef broth
- 2 tbsp Worcestershire sauce

Instructions:

1. Mix dry ingredients and rub over brisket. Let rest for 2 hours.
2. Preheat smoker to 110°C.
3. Smoke brisket for 6-8 hours, spritzing with broth and Worcestershire every hour.
4. Wrap in foil and cook for another 2 hours until tender.

Dark Chocolate Chili

Ingredients:

- 500g ground beef
- 1 onion, diced
- 3 garlic cloves, minced
- 1 can (400g) black beans, drained
- 1 can (400g) crushed tomatoes
- 1 tbsp chili powder
- 1 tsp smoked paprika
- 1 tbsp unsweetened cocoa powder
- ½ tsp cinnamon
- 1 tbsp brown sugar
- ½ tsp salt
- 250ml beef broth

Instructions:

1. Brown beef in a pot, then add onion and garlic.
2. Stir in spices, cocoa, and sugar.
3. Add tomatoes, beans, and broth. Simmer for 1 hour.

Black Garlic Butter Chicken

Ingredients:

- 4 chicken thighs, bone-in
- 2 tbsp butter
- 4 cloves black garlic, mashed
- 1 tbsp soy sauce
- 1 tsp honey
- ½ tsp black pepper
- ½ tsp smoked paprika

Instructions:

1. Preheat oven to 200°C.
2. Mix butter, black garlic, soy sauce, honey, and spices.
3. Rub onto chicken thighs and bake for 35–40 minutes.

Mystery Meatloaf

Ingredients:

- 500g ground beef
- 1 egg
- ½ cup breadcrumbs
- 1 tbsp Worcestershire sauce
- 2 tbsp black garlic, minced
- ½ cup black olives, chopped
- 1 tsp smoked paprika
- ½ tsp black pepper

Instructions:

1. Preheat oven to 180°C.
2. Mix all ingredients and form into a loaf.
3. Bake for 45–50 minutes.

Pitch-Black Squid Ink Pasta

Ingredients:

- 250g squid ink pasta
- 2 tbsp olive oil
- 3 garlic cloves, minced
- 200g shrimp, cleaned
- ½ tsp chili flakes
- 100ml white wine
- 2 tbsp squid ink
- ½ lemon, juiced
- Salt and pepper to taste

Instructions:

1. Cook pasta according to instructions.
2. Heat oil, sauté garlic and shrimp.
3. Add chili, wine, and squid ink. Stir in pasta and lemon juice.

Hidden Ingredient Casserole

Ingredients:

- 500g ground beef
- 1 onion, chopped
- 2 cloves garlic, minced
- 1 can (400g) black beans
- 1 cup cooked rice
- ½ cup black olives, chopped
- 1 tsp smoked paprika
- 1 tsp cumin
- 200g shredded cheese
- 2 tbsp balsamic vinegar

Instructions:

1. Preheat oven to 180°C.
2. Brown beef with onion and garlic.
3. Mix with other ingredients and transfer to a baking dish.
4. Top with cheese and bake for 25 minutes.

Twilight Truffle Risotto

Ingredients:

- 1 cup Arborio rice
- 2 tbsp butter
- ½ onion, diced
- 2 garlic cloves, minced
- 750ml chicken broth, warmed
- 2 tbsp black truffle paste
- 50g Parmesan cheese, grated

Instructions:

1. Sauté onion and garlic in butter.
2. Add rice, then slowly add broth while stirring.
3. Once creamy, stir in truffle paste and Parmesan.

Charcoal-Grilled Lamb Chops

Ingredients:

- 4 lamb chops
- 2 tbsp olive oil
- 1 tbsp blackened spice mix
- ½ tsp sea salt
- ½ tsp black pepper

Instructions:

1. Rub lamb with oil and spices.
2. Grill over high heat for 3 minutes per side.

Obsidian Glazed Ribs

Ingredients:

- 1 rack pork ribs
- 2 tbsp soy sauce
- 1 tbsp balsamic vinegar
- 2 tbsp honey
- 1 tsp black garlic paste
- 1 tsp smoked paprika

Instructions:

1. Preheat oven to 160°C.
2. Mix glaze and coat ribs.
3. Bake for 2 hours, brushing with glaze every 30 minutes.

Nocturnal Mushroom Soup

Ingredients:

- 2 tbsp butter
- 1 onion, diced
- 3 garlic cloves, minced
- 500g mixed mushrooms, sliced
- 1 tsp black garlic paste
- 750ml vegetable broth
- 200ml heavy cream
- ½ tsp black pepper
- Salt to taste

Instructions:

1. Sauté onion and garlic in butter until soft.
2. Add mushrooms and cook until browned.
3. Stir in black garlic and broth. Simmer for 20 minutes.
4. Blend until smooth, then stir in cream.

Phantom Pepper Stir-Fry

Ingredients:

- 2 tbsp vegetable oil
- 1 bell pepper, sliced
- 1 red chili, chopped
- 200g beef or tofu, sliced
- 2 cloves garlic, minced
- 1 tbsp soy sauce
- 1 tsp ghost pepper hot sauce
- 1 tsp black pepper

Instructions:

1. Heat oil in a pan and stir-fry beef or tofu.
2. Add peppers, garlic, and sauces.
3. Stir-fry for 3–5 minutes.

Secret Spice Meatballs

Ingredients:

- 500g ground beef
- 1 egg
- ½ cup breadcrumbs
- 2 tbsp black garlic paste
- 1 tsp smoked paprika
- ½ tsp cayenne
- 1 tsp salt
- 1 tsp black pepper

Instructions:

1. Preheat oven to 180°C.
2. Mix ingredients and form meatballs.
3. Bake for 20 minutes.

Dusky Bourbon-Braised Short Ribs

Ingredients:

- 1kg short ribs
- 1 tbsp olive oil
- 1 onion, chopped
- 3 garlic cloves, minced
- 250ml bourbon
- 500ml beef broth
- 2 tbsp balsamic vinegar
- 1 tsp smoked paprika
- Salt and pepper to taste

Instructions:

1. Sear ribs in oil, then remove.
2. Sauté onion and garlic, then deglaze with bourbon.
3. Add broth, vinegar, and spices. Return ribs and braise at 160°C for 3 hours.

Starlit Black Bean Burgers

Ingredients:

- 1 can (400g) black beans, drained
- ½ cup breadcrumbs
- 1 egg
- 1 tsp cumin
- 1 tsp smoked paprika
- ½ tsp garlic powder
- Salt and pepper to taste

Instructions:

1. Mash beans and mix with other ingredients.
2. Form patties and pan-fry for 3 minutes per side.

Cloaked-in-Darkness Beef Stew

Ingredients:

- 500g beef chuck, cubed
- 1 tbsp olive oil
- 1 onion, chopped
- 3 garlic cloves, minced
- 2 tbsp tomato paste
- 500ml stout beer
- 500ml beef broth
- 1 can (400g) black beans
- 2 carrots, chopped
- 1 tbsp Worcestershire sauce
- 1 tsp smoked paprika

Instructions:

1. Brown beef in oil, then remove.
2. Sauté onion, garlic, and tomato paste.
3. Add beer, broth, and remaining ingredients. Simmer for 2 hours.

Enigma Eggplant Parmesan

Ingredients:

- 1 large eggplant, sliced
- 1 cup breadcrumbs
- 1 egg, beaten
- 1 cup marinara sauce
- 100g mozzarella, shredded
- 50g Parmesan, grated

Instructions:

1. Dip eggplant slices in egg, then coat with breadcrumbs.
2. Bake at 180°C for 20 minutes.
3. Layer with marinara and cheeses, then bake for 15 more minutes.

Blackened Cajun Salmon

Ingredients:

- 2 salmon fillets
- 1 tbsp olive oil
- 1 tbsp Cajun seasoning
- ½ tsp smoked paprika
- ½ tsp black pepper

Instructions:

1. Coat salmon with oil and seasonings.
2. Sear in a hot pan for 3 minutes per side.

Deep Midnight Pot Roast

Ingredients:

- 1.5kg beef roast
- 2 tbsp olive oil
- 1 onion, chopped
- 3 garlic cloves, minced
- 500ml beef broth
- 250ml red wine
- 2 tbsp Worcestershire sauce
- 1 tsp smoked paprika

Instructions:

1. Sear beef in oil, then remove.
2. Sauté onion and garlic, then add liquids and spices.
3. Return beef and roast at 160°C for 3 hours.

Hidden Heat Tandoori Chicken

Ingredients:

- 4 chicken thighs
- 1 cup yogurt
- 2 tbsp lemon juice
- 1 tbsp tandoori spice mix
- ½ tsp cayenne
- Salt to taste

Instructions:

1. Marinate chicken in yogurt, lemon juice, and spices for 2 hours.
2. Grill or bake at 200°C for 30 minutes.

Shadowy Smoked Mac & Cheese

Ingredients:

- 250g elbow macaroni
- 2 tbsp butter
- 2 tbsp flour
- 500ml whole milk
- 200g smoked cheddar, shredded
- 100g gouda, shredded
- 1 tsp smoked paprika
- ½ tsp black pepper
- ½ cup panko breadcrumbs
- 2 tbsp melted butter

Instructions:

1. Cook macaroni according to package instructions.
2. Melt butter in a pan, whisk in flour, and cook for 1 minute.
3. Slowly whisk in milk and simmer until thickened.
4. Stir in cheeses, paprika, and pepper.
5. Toss macaroni with sauce, transfer to a baking dish, and top with buttered panko.
6. Bake at 180°C for 20 minutes until golden.

Eclipse Espresso BBQ Chicken

Ingredients:

- 4 chicken thighs
- 1 tbsp olive oil
- 1 tbsp espresso powder
- 1 tbsp brown sugar
- 1 tsp smoked paprika
- 1 tsp chili powder
- ½ tsp black pepper
- ½ tsp salt
- ½ cup BBQ sauce

Instructions:

1. Mix espresso, sugar, spices, and oil to form a rub.
2. Coat chicken and let marinate for 1 hour.
3. Grill or bake at 200°C for 30 minutes, brushing with BBQ sauce in the last 10 minutes.

Forbidden Rice & Coconut Curry

Ingredients:

- 1 cup black (forbidden) rice
- 1 tbsp coconut oil
- 1 onion, diced
- 2 garlic cloves, minced
- 1 tbsp curry paste
- 1 can (400ml) coconut milk
- 1 cup vegetable broth
- 1 sweet potato, cubed
- 1 cup chickpeas, drained
- Salt to taste

Instructions:

1. Cook black rice according to package instructions.
2. Sauté onion and garlic in coconut oil.
3. Stir in curry paste, then add coconut milk and broth.
4. Add sweet potato and chickpeas, simmer until tender.
5. Serve over black rice.

Smoldering Ember Meat Pie

Ingredients:

- 500g ground beef
- 1 onion, chopped
- 2 garlic cloves, minced
- 1 tbsp Worcestershire sauce
- 1 tsp smoked paprika
- ½ tsp cayenne
- ½ tsp black pepper
- 1 cup beef broth
- 1 tbsp flour
- 1 sheet puff pastry
- 1 egg, beaten

Instructions:

1. Sauté beef, onion, and garlic until browned.
2. Stir in spices, Worcestershire, and flour.
3. Add broth and simmer until thickened.
4. Transfer to a pie dish, cover with puff pastry, brush with egg, and bake at 190°C for 25 minutes.

Midnight Market Noodle Bowl

Ingredients:

- 200g ramen noodles
- 1 tbsp sesame oil
- 1 garlic clove, minced
- 1 tbsp soy sauce
- 1 tbsp oyster sauce
- ½ tsp black vinegar
- 1 tsp chili flakes
- 1 green onion, sliced
- 1 soft-boiled egg, halved

Instructions:

1. Cook noodles and drain.
2. Sauté garlic in sesame oil, then add sauces and chili flakes.
3. Toss noodles in sauce and serve with green onion and egg.

Candied Bacon Mystery Bites

Ingredients:

- 8 slices bacon
- ¼ cup brown sugar
- ½ tsp cayenne
- ½ tsp black pepper

Instructions:

1. Coat bacon in sugar and spices.
2. Bake at 180°C for 20 minutes until crispy.

Sable-Spiced Lentil Soup

Ingredients:

- 1 tbsp olive oil
- 1 onion, diced
- 2 garlic cloves, minced
- 1 tsp cumin
- ½ tsp smoked paprika
- 1 cup black lentils
- 1 can (400ml) diced tomatoes
- 750ml vegetable broth
- Salt and pepper to taste

Instructions:

1. Sauté onion and garlic in oil.
2. Stir in spices, lentils, tomatoes, and broth.
3. Simmer for 30 minutes.

Moonlit Moroccan Tagine

Ingredients:

- 1 tbsp olive oil
- 500g lamb, cubed
- 1 onion, chopped
- 2 garlic cloves, minced
- 1 tsp cinnamon
- 1 tsp cumin
- ½ tsp smoked paprika
- ½ cup dried apricots, chopped
- 500ml beef broth

Instructions:

1. Brown lamb in oil.
2. Add onion, garlic, and spices.
3. Stir in apricots and broth.
4. Simmer for 1 hour until tender.

Dark Roast Coffee-Rubbed Steak

Ingredients:

- 2 steaks
- 1 tbsp ground coffee
- 1 tsp brown sugar
- 1 tsp black pepper
- ½ tsp salt
- ½ tsp smoked paprika

Instructions:

1. Mix dry ingredients and rub onto steaks.
2. Let sit for 30 minutes.
3. Sear for 3 minutes per side, then rest for 5 minutes.

Dusky Plum-Glazed Duck

Ingredients:

- 2 duck breasts
- 1 tbsp olive oil
- ½ cup plum jam
- 1 tbsp balsamic vinegar
- 1 tsp soy sauce
- ½ tsp black pepper

Instructions:

1. Score duck skin and sear for 5 minutes.
2. Flip and cook for 3 minutes.
3. Heat jam, vinegar, soy sauce, and pepper to form glaze.
4. Brush onto duck and cook for 2 more minutes.

Pitch-Black Charcoal Pizza

Ingredients:

- 250g all-purpose flour
- 1 tbsp activated charcoal powder
- 1 tsp salt
- 1 tsp sugar
- 1 packet (7g) instant yeast
- 150ml warm water
- 1 tbsp olive oil
- ½ cup tomato sauce
- 150g mozzarella cheese, shredded
- 100g black olives, sliced
- 100g mushrooms, sliced
- ½ tsp dried oregano

Instructions:

1. Mix flour, charcoal, salt, sugar, and yeast.
2. Add warm water and olive oil, knead until smooth.
3. Let dough rise for 1 hour.
4. Roll out, spread tomato sauce, and add toppings.
5. Bake at 220°C for 12-15 minutes.

Unknown Depths Seafood Gumbo

Ingredients:

- 2 tbsp butter
- 2 tbsp flour
- 1 onion, diced
- 1 bell pepper, diced
- 2 celery stalks, diced
- 2 garlic cloves, minced
- 500ml seafood stock
- 1 can (400g) diced tomatoes
- 200g shrimp, peeled
- 200g crab meat
- 1 tsp Cajun seasoning
- ½ tsp smoked paprika
- ½ tsp black pepper

Instructions:

1. Make a roux by cooking butter and flour until golden.
2. Add onion, pepper, celery, and garlic. Cook until soft.
3. Stir in stock, tomatoes, and seasonings. Simmer for 20 minutes.
4. Add seafood and cook for 5 minutes.

Sinister Smoked Pork Shoulder

Ingredients:

- 1.5kg pork shoulder
- 2 tbsp smoked paprika
- 1 tbsp garlic powder
- 1 tbsp onion powder
- 1 tbsp brown sugar
- 1 tsp cayenne pepper
- 1 tsp salt
- 1 tsp black pepper
- 2 tbsp mustard

Instructions:

1. Rub pork with mustard, then coat with spices.
2. Let marinate for 4 hours or overnight.
3. Smoke at 120°C for 6-8 hours, until tender.

Shrouded in Smoke BBQ Wings

Ingredients:

- 1kg chicken wings
- 1 tbsp olive oil
- 1 tbsp smoked paprika
- 1 tsp garlic powder
- ½ tsp salt
- ½ tsp black pepper
- ½ cup BBQ sauce

Instructions:

1. Toss wings with oil and seasonings.
2. Bake at 200°C for 30 minutes, flipping halfway.
3. Toss in BBQ sauce and bake for 5 more minutes.

Cloaked Cauliflower Mash

Ingredients:

- 1 head cauliflower, chopped
- 2 tbsp butter
- ¼ cup heavy cream
- 1 garlic clove, minced
- Salt & pepper to taste

Instructions:

1. Steam cauliflower until soft.
2. Blend with butter, cream, garlic, salt, and pepper.

Hidden Treasure Jambalaya

Ingredients:

- 2 tbsp olive oil
- 1 onion, diced
- 1 bell pepper, diced
- 2 celery stalks, chopped
- 2 garlic cloves, minced
- 1 cup long-grain rice
- 500ml chicken broth
- 1 can (400g) diced tomatoes
- 200g smoked sausage, sliced
- 200g shrimp, peeled
- 1 tsp Cajun seasoning

Instructions:

1. Sauté onion, bell pepper, and celery in oil.
2. Stir in garlic, rice, and broth.
3. Add tomatoes, sausage, and seasoning. Simmer for 15 minutes.
4. Stir in shrimp and cook for 5 more minutes.

Silent Night Szechuan Noodles

Ingredients:

- 200g noodles
- 1 tbsp sesame oil
- 1 tbsp soy sauce
- 1 tbsp Szechuan peppercorns, ground
- 1 tsp chili flakes
- 1 garlic clove, minced
- 1 green onion, sliced

Instructions:

1. Cook noodles and drain.
2. Heat sesame oil, sauté garlic, and add spices.
3. Toss noodles in sauce and top with green onions.

Dark Honey-Glazed Ham

Ingredients:

- 1.5kg ham
- ½ cup honey
- ¼ cup soy sauce
- 1 tbsp Dijon mustard
- 1 tsp black pepper

Instructions:

1. Mix honey, soy sauce, mustard, and pepper.
2. Score ham and brush with glaze.
3. Bake at 180°C for 1 hour, basting every 15 minutes.

Mystery Mushroom Stroganoff

Ingredients:

- 2 tbsp butter
- 1 onion, chopped
- 250g mushrooms, sliced
- 2 garlic cloves, minced
- 1 tbsp flour
- 1 cup beef broth
- ½ cup sour cream
- Salt & pepper to taste
- 200g egg noodles

Instructions:

1. Sauté onion, mushrooms, and garlic in butter.
2. Stir in flour, then broth. Simmer until thickened.
3. Stir in sour cream and seasonings.
4. Serve over egg noodles.

Veiled Vanilla-Balsamic Chicken

Ingredients:

- 2 chicken breasts
- 2 tbsp balsamic vinegar
- 1 tbsp vanilla extract
- 1 tbsp olive oil
- 1 garlic clove, minced
- 1 tsp Dijon mustard
- Salt & pepper to taste

Instructions:

1. Mix balsamic, vanilla, olive oil, garlic, mustard, salt, and pepper.
2. Marinate chicken for at least 1 hour.
3. Sear in a pan over medium heat for 6-7 minutes per side.

Black Bean & Chorizo Enchiladas

Ingredients:

- 1 cup black beans, cooked
- 200g chorizo, crumbled
- 1 cup shredded cheese
- 8 small tortillas
- 1 cup enchilada sauce

Instructions:

1. Cook chorizo, then mix with black beans.
2. Fill tortillas, roll, and place in a baking dish.
3. Top with enchilada sauce and cheese.
4. Bake at 180°C for 20 minutes.

Mysterious Midnight Lasagna

Ingredients:

- 200g ground beef
- 1 onion, chopped
- 2 garlic cloves, minced
- 1 can (400g) crushed tomatoes
- 1 tsp Italian seasoning
- 250g ricotta cheese
- 250g mozzarella, shredded
- 6 lasagna sheets

Instructions:

1. Sauté onion, garlic, and beef. Add tomatoes and seasonings.
2. Layer sauce, lasagna sheets, ricotta, and mozzarella.
3. Bake at 180°C for 40 minutes.

Obscured in Darkness Ramen

Ingredients:

- 2 packs ramen noodles
- 4 cups chicken broth
- 1 tbsp soy sauce
- 1 tsp sesame oil
- 1 garlic clove, minced
- 1 soft-boiled egg
- 50g mushrooms, sliced

Instructions:

1. Cook garlic in sesame oil. Add broth and soy sauce.
2. Simmer, then add mushrooms and ramen.
3. Serve with a soft-boiled egg.

Shadowy Shepherd's Pie

Ingredients:

- 250g ground lamb
- 1 onion, diced
- 1 carrot, diced
- 1 cup mashed potatoes
- 1 tbsp Worcestershire sauce
- ½ tsp thyme
- Salt & pepper to taste

Instructions:

1. Cook lamb with onion and carrot. Add Worcestershire, thyme, salt, and pepper.
2. Transfer to a baking dish, top with mashed potatoes.
3. Bake at 180°C for 25 minutes.

Deep Night Bourbon Caramel Pork

Ingredients:

- 500g pork tenderloin
- 2 tbsp bourbon
- 2 tbsp brown sugar
- 1 tbsp butter
- 1 tsp salt

Instructions:

1. Sear pork in a pan.
2. Melt butter, stir in brown sugar and bourbon.
3. Brush glaze on pork and bake at 190°C for 20 minutes.

Masquerade Meat & Cheese Fondue

Ingredients:

- 200g Gruyère cheese, grated
- 200g cheddar, grated
- 1 garlic clove, minced
- ½ cup white wine
- 1 tsp cornstarch
- 200g cooked meats and bread cubes

Instructions:

1. Melt cheese with wine and garlic. Stir in cornstarch.
2. Serve with meats and bread cubes for dipping.

Lurking Lobster Bisque

Ingredients:

- 2 lobster tails
- 2 tbsp butter
- 1 shallot, diced
- 1 garlic clove, minced
- 1 cup heavy cream
- 2 cups seafood stock
- Salt & pepper to taste

Instructions:

1. Sauté shallot and garlic in butter.
2. Add stock and cream. Simmer.
3. Stir in chopped lobster meat.

Blindfolded Brown Butter Gnocchi

Ingredients:

- 250g gnocchi
- 3 tbsp butter
- 1 tsp sage
- Salt & pepper to taste

Instructions:

1. Cook gnocchi, drain.
2. Brown butter in a pan, add sage.
3. Toss gnocchi in sauce.

Hidden Hands Spicy Curry

Ingredients:

- 200g chicken, cubed
- 1 onion, chopped
- 2 garlic cloves, minced
- 1 tbsp curry powder
- 1 cup coconut milk
- ½ tsp chili flakes

Instructions:

1. Cook onion and garlic. Add chicken and curry powder.
2. Pour in coconut milk and chili flakes. Simmer.

Secret Smokehouse Brisket

Ingredients:

- 1kg beef brisket
- 2 tbsp smoked paprika
- 1 tbsp salt
- 1 tbsp black pepper
- 1 tsp garlic powder

Instructions:

1. Rub brisket with spices.
2. Smoke at 120°C for 8 hours.

www.ingramcontent.com/pod-product-compliance
Lightning Source LLC
LaVergne TN
LVHW081334060526
838201LV00055B/2635